LOOKING **BACK**

WORK

PHILIP SAUVAIN

Wayland

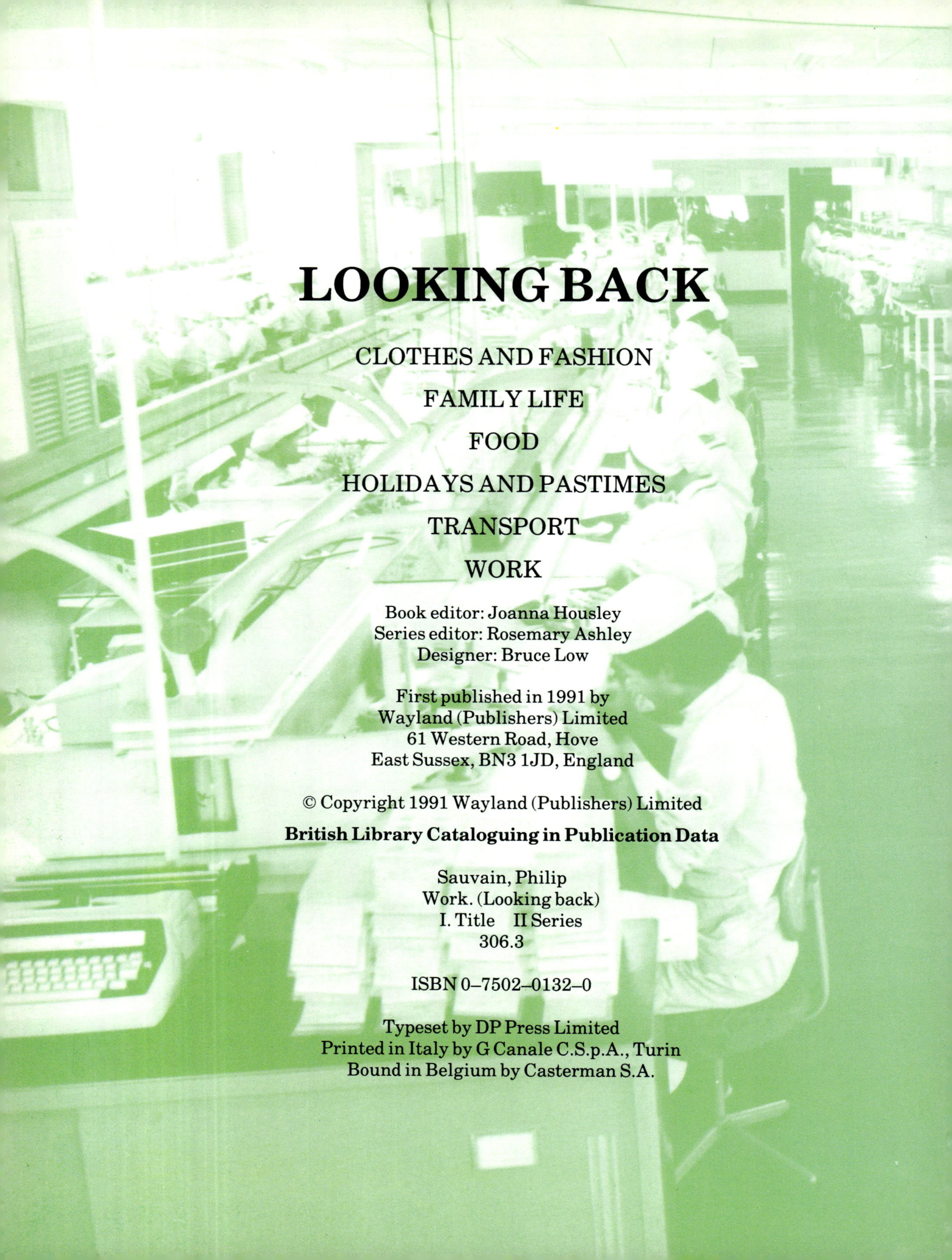

LOOKING BACK

CLOTHES AND FASHION

FAMILY LIFE

FOOD

HOLIDAYS AND PASTIMES

TRANSPORT

WORK

Book editor: Joanna Housley
Series editor: Rosemary Ashley
Designer: Bruce Low

First published in 1991 by
Wayland (Publishers) Limited
61 Western Road, Hove
East Sussex, BN3 1JD, England

British Library Cataloguing in Publication Data

Sauvain, Philip
Work. (Looking back)
I. Title II Series
306.3

ISBN 0–7502–0132–0

Typeset by DP Press Limited
Printed in Italy by G Canale C.S.p.A., Turin
Bound in Belgium by Casterman S.A.

CONTENTS

INTRODUCTION

If you had been a child in 1900, you could have left school at the age of twelve. Children who went out to work then had little choice of job. Most went to work in a shop, farm or factory near their home. A Lancashire cotton worker said he 'started at 12 years old half-time'. This meant going half a day to work in the mill and half a day to school.

People worked long hours for low pay in those days. Their places of work were often noisy, dark, dusty, damp and either too cold or too hot. Accidents were common and visitors to factory towns often saw crippled people in the streets.

Since 1900, there have been many improvements. People today work a shorter working week. They enjoy longer holidays and are better paid. Accidents are rare. People wear protective clothing at work if they need it. If they lose their jobs, they can get unemployment benefit from the government and compensation from their employers.

Textile mills were hot, dusty and noisy in the early 1900s.

We often take improvements like these for granted. But people had to stand up for these rights in the past to get the better working conditions which everyone enjoys today. Women had to fight for equal pay for equal work and the right to be treated in the same way as men at work.

Other changes came about because of two world wars. Some changes came about because foreign workers made goods, such as cotton cloth, more cheaply than in Britain. There were over a million cotton workers in Lancashire in 1900. Today there are fewer than 40,000.

In 1925, Fleet Street printing presses required plenty of men to operate them.

Computers and automatic machines do work nowadays which used to be done by hundreds of thousands of people in the past. Tractors and combine harvesters have replaced a million farm workers. Washing machines, dishwashers, food mixers, motor mowers and vacuum cleaners have taken the place of servants.

In this noisy, modern factory, workers wear headphones to protect their ears.

1 THE EARLY YEARS

At haytime in 1900, people in the countryside could see long lines of farm workers in the fields, cutting grass with their scythes. Most working people had manual jobs like this. They worked with their hands.

Farm work was backbreaking and poorly paid. During the first years of the twentieth century, British farmers were losing money because cheaper food could be bought from other countries. Wages fell, and by 1911 four out of five English people lived and worked in towns rather than in the countryside.

Farm workers looking for jobs had to go to a hiring fair to get work. A Yorkshire farm worker said it was like 'a slave market'. He left school at the age of thirteen-and-a-half and was hired out to a farmer for £12 for one year. Even then he was better off than 'gangers'. These were boys and girls organized into 'gangs', who were hired out to farmers to work in the fields. Gangers were often badly treated and always badly paid.

Working-class women in the towns had long been used to working in mills and factories. By 1900 a growing number of better-off women were also looking for work. Many got jobs as typists, telephonists or as assistants in the new department stores.

In those days shop assistants served each customer in person. Most foods were sold loose from big containers, such as those which held tea and sugar. This meant that everything had to be

Farm workers did most jobs by hand in the early years of the century. It was very hard work.

By the early 1900s, women were beginning to find work in offices.

measured out, weighed and packed by hand. Liquids, such as vinegar, were kept in casks and poured directly into bottles supplied by the customer. Soap was cut into slices from a long block.

Shop assistants often took great pride in their work. A Rochdale man said, 'Everybody in the street knew you were working at the Co-op. You were treated like royalty. Everybody said, "He's working at the Co-op." ' An assistant in a London department store remembered that they had to dress like 'proper little gentlemen'. They wore 'black jackets, striped trousers,

Sarah, aged 91, recalled her work as a servant in the early years of the century.

'My first place? I didn't stop there long. It was a shilling [5p] a day. They didn't give you enough food. I only stayed about three months. The other girl was dirty that had been there before. There was a surround to the fireplace and it was just black bright. So I used to wash it every day to try and get it a bit cleaner. And the woman who employed me says, "Who learned you how to clean?" I think they were glad to be rid of this other one!'

The fabric department of Peter Robinson's store in 1910, where customers were served in comfortable surroundings.

black shoes, stiff white collar and a sober-coloured tie'. The shop walkers (supervisors) wore morning dress. 'The head shop walker was a god. We were all scared stiff of him.'

It was not an easy life. Nearly half a million shop assistants had to live above the shop in which they worked. They worked very long hours. Friday and Saturday nights were the busiest times. Most workers had been paid by then and the streets were crowded. Shops stayed open until 8.00 or 9.00 in the evening. Some did not close until midnight. Although this made shopping easier for the customer, it was hard work for the shop assistants. In 1911 their plight was recognized by the government, and an act was passed by Parliament making it compulsory for shops to close one half day in the working week.

Working life was no easier for the servant. Some very rich families employed as many as a hundred servants. There were housekeepers, nannies, cooks, maids, gardeners, footmen, chauffeurs and butlers. Even people living in small houses could afford to employ a servant to wash, cook and clean. This was because servants' wages were very low.

Jane Robinson worked as a servant in a vicarage in the early 1900s.

'We didn't have much time off. It was my job to bath the three children and 'do' at night. I lived with my cousin. She was cook and I was housemaid. We'd get up about half-six. They had a gardener too but he went off to War in 1914. It was my job to set the table and take stuff in. Woe betide you if you left a spoon behind. The bell used to go. "Robinson! You've left a spoon!" They'd have a fit today!'

Interviewed in 1990

Wealthy ladies had maids to help them dress in the early years of this century.

2 INDUSTRY BEFORE 1914

Working conditions were even worse for people in the small back-street factories of cities like London and Manchester. There, working women and children crowded into dirty, badly-lit rooms to make hats and clothes. Sweatshops like these exploited the workers. Rates of pay were very low and the risk of injury and bad health was often great.

In 1901 a Lancashire firm admitted paying only 1s 2d (6p) a day to seven women and two girls. They had been forced to work until 11.00 one night and until 2.00 in the morning on another. The magistrate asked, 'Do you mean to say you pay less than a farthing an hour to these women?' The manager replied, 'Yes. The women started work at 6.30 am

Young children often went out to work at the beginning of the century. Their wages helped to keep many families from starving.

In the 1900s a grocery store like this needed many shop assistants.

and on this occasion would have worked until 9 o'clock [in the evening].'

Noise was one of the main nuisances at work. In the textile mills of Lancashire and Yorkshire it could be deafening and could go on all day long. 'A grinding, screeching noise' complained one visitor. He went on: 'The whole place vibrates. The heat is very great, and the air is full of a yellow, noisome dust. And the smell – the horror of it when it comes to you through the woolsorting factories, from the heated rooms in which the wool is scoured of the grease.'

Workers worked long shifts. In northern mill towns they were often woken by a 'knocker-up'. *'Five loud strokes from the Town Hall clock. Here and there a man may be seen carrying a long pole, having a kind of mop made of thin wires at one end. Up and down the long street he goes, stopping here and there, in some streets at nearly every house, and applying his mop to the bedroom window-pane. A hailstorm of sound results, calculated to wake the dead.'*

Ada Nield Chew in *The Englishwoman*, July 1912

Coal-mining was dirty, hard and dangerous work in the 1900s.

Robert Sherard was a journalist who wrote about working conditions. When he visited chemical works at Widnes and St Helens near Liverpool, he said he saw 'numerous and fine children' but never saw 'any old people'. He claimed this was because chemical workers were always at risk of sudden death or accident. Those who survived had to breathe in foul gases from the many chemical works in the area. They rotted 'the clothes, the teeth, and, in the end, the bodies of the workers'. Every tree and blade of grass was dead for miles around. One of the workers had black stumps for teeth. They were

Coal-miners worked on their knees or on their sides in the darkness of a pit for eight or ten hours at a time.

'I have been down coal-mines 1,000 feet below the surface, mines into which there is running a constant stream of water; I have crawled for a couple of miles till my back has ached; I have tramped slush, and been choked with fumes.

J.F. Fraser,
'Life in a Coal Mine',
Windsor Magazine, 1897.

so bad he could not eat the crusts on bread. This man told Sherard that he stood eight hours on end in front of a fiery furnace every day. The heat was so intense that he had to have two towels to mop up the sweat.

Yet other Cheshire chemical workers, at Port Sunlight, lived in clean, modern surroundings in newly-built semi-detached houses with large gardens. These had been built especially for the workers.

Some factory owners built model housing estates like this one at Port Sunlight in Cheshire.

3 WORK IN WARTIME

Big changes came for people at work in August 1914, when Britain went to war with Germany. Mills, mines and farms were soon short of workers as millions of men joined the army. Many factories were forced to employ women in jobs which had previously been thought suitable only for men.

But the new recruits soon proved they could do the same jobs as well as the men. There were women bus conductors and farm workers. Women drove trucks and cranes. They swept chimneys and stoked furnaces. They made guns, shells and bombs. Children, too, played their part in 'working for victory'.

Women workers made guns, bombs and shells in the First World War.

Doctors and nurses looked after wounded soldiers on the battlefronts and at home.

George Robinson left school at thirteen just before the War. He was too young to join the army but his work was vital to the war effort since he made weapons. He can still remember the day he got his job.

'I went up to the steel works seeking a job. I called at the office. I said, "Any chance of a job, Mister?" The boss replied, "Aye. It's a twelve-hour day. You can start at six in the morning or six at night."

When I first went there, they were making shells of course. I went in 1914. I did a man's job straight away because they were taking men out of there for the War.'

Interviewed in 1990

Accidents were common. George Robinson remembers one accident in the steel rolling mill where he worked. 'There were two of these girls setting rolls – the rollers that took the red hot ingots through. A fellow was stood at the bottom and was burned.' On another occasion he saw 'a man get his hair caught in cogs. Took off half his head.'

These accidents made a deep impression on the young boy. 'They killed one a week in those days you know. They were forced to make changes about 1920.' Seventy-five years later George can still point to a reminder of the old days. 'I've a lump in my eye myself. A lump of steel. They couldn't get it out. You can see it in there. It's buried in.'

One result of the labour shortage was that wages rose considerably during the War. A shipyard worker earning £1.90 a week in 1914 earned £3.70 in 1918. A bricklayer's wages went up from £1.45 a week to £3.25. However, even though women did the same work as men, they were not paid the same wages.

Wartime farmers were asked to produce as much food from the land as possible.

George Robinson's wife also worked during the War. She had a job as a dairymaid, making cheese. 'It was all done by hand. You put rennet in and then set it. It went into a sort of jelly. And then you had to keep going round and round. You had to roll your sleeve right up to here. They wouldn't do that today.' Her most vivid memory of the War came on 11 November 1918. 'They gave us a golden half sovereign then for working on Peace Day,' she recalls.

But they did not give her a job after the War. The hundreds of thousands of women who had volunteered for work in 1914–18 had to give their jobs back to the returning soldiers. Most thought at first that the War had hardly changed anything.

George Robinson remembers how strict his employers were about their workers arriving on time:
'When you clocked in on a morning they used to allow you one minute. If it were 6.02, you had quarter of an hour's money stopped. There were twelve-hour shifts when I first started. Eight-hour shift didn't come in while [until] the 1920s. And no holiday for pay in those days you know. We worked New Year's Day.'
Interviewed in 1990

Women took over the men's jobs while they were away at the Front.

4 IN AND OUT OF WORK

After the First World War people's attitudes to work changed. Women had had a taste of freedom. They no longer wanted to work as servants, being told what to do by someone else. Soldiers who had faced death in the trenches wanted better working conditions in their jobs. In 1926 a million coal-miners went on strike with the slogan: 'Not a penny off the pay! Not a minute on the day!' This was because the pit owners were trying to lower wages and make the working day longer. At first the miners got help from workers in other industries. But a General Strike of all workers in May 1926 ended after only nine days.

Soldiers handing back their service kit in 1918.

Volunteers drove buses and even trains during the General Strike in 1926.

The dole queue was a common sight in the 1920s and 1930s.

Many of these workers later lost their jobs for good in the years of depression that followed the collapse of the New York stock exchange in October 1929. In those days unemployed workers were paid a small allowance, the dole, by the government. How much you were paid depended on where you lived. A 55-year-old pottery worker got only eight shillings (40p) a week in 1933. This was because his daughters lived with him and they both had jobs. On Christmas Day, he stubbornly refused to eat any chicken or ham – because they had bought it, not him.

The magazine *Picture Post* told the story of one man looking for work in 1939. It called him 'The Picture of our Time: Alone, Walking for Miles, Trying to Find

Life for many unemployed workers was made all the harder because the places where they lived had been spoiled by industry in the past. This was a colliery waste tip near Durham in 1933.

'Its vast dark bulk, steaming and smoking at various levels, blotted out all the landscape at the back of the village. Its lowest slope was only a few yards from the miserable cluster of houses. The whole village and everybody in it was buried in this thick reek, was smothered in ashes and sulphuric fumes. Wherever I stood they made me gasp and cough.'

J.B. Priestley, *English Journey*

a Job. Unemployed, he lives on the charity of the State, which cannot find him work. But he wants to work, to be a man, not a number on a Ministry of Labour card. He is one of nearly 2,000,000.'

Working conditions took a long time to improve. Over 5,000 miners were killed and 800,000 injured between 1927 and 1931. Because of the slump in business, many manufacturers did not have the money to buy the latest or the safest machines. Coal-miners still cut coal by hand at a time when American and German miners used coal-cutting machines.

Cotton mills were little better. A spinner said they were 'noisy, oily, dusty and like a prison, and very hot'. Another said, 'You could always smell the weaving on your clothes and in your hair.'

The factory chimney looms over nearby houses.

In the 1920s British miners still cut coal by hand.

Women who worked at the pithead – sorting coal on a conveyor belt – found the work as tough as that of the men below ground.

'It was hard work and these belts was rolling all the time. There were about twenty-four of us with two belts There were twelve to each belt, six at one side and six at the other, about a yard apart. And in the winter time when it was very cold, the wind used to come bustling through and your fingertips used to be raw you know 'cos coal is hard.'

Jane Carroll, screen hand at a colliery, interviewed for the BBC Television series *All Our Working Lives: Coal*, 1984

Shops like Woolworth provided many new jobs in the 1930s.

Workers left for home looking like snowmen covered in cotton. A cotton winder remembered the amount of standing she had to do. 'You was on your feet all the time. You never sat down.'

By contrast, many of the people working in the Midlands and in the South were much better off. You could tell this from the shops. Chain stores were doing very well. Woolworth and Marks and Spencer were opening new branches almost every week in the 1930s.

Cadbury's employees could enjoy unusually pleasant surroundings.

People could get jobs in the new factories which made motor cars, radios and domestic appliances. Some people moved from the North to get jobs in the South. Over 2,000 Ford workers left Manchester in 1931 to work in the new Ford Motor Works at Dagenham in Essex.

Many of these firms looked after their employees very well indeed. Cadbury's built splendid playing fields and sports pavilions at their chocolate works at Bournville near Birmingham. There was even a large concert hall where concerts were held at midday. J.B. Priestley said, 'The factory is almost as busy in the evenings as it is in the daytime. Games, music, drama, lectures, classes, hobbies, conferences, all keep the place in full swing.'

5 FULL EMPLOYMENT

In 1938, Parliament passed a law giving millions of workers the right to a holiday with pay each year. In the last summer before the Second World War (1939–45), thousands of factory workers enjoyed their first holidays by the sea.

The War itself solved many of the problems of the 1930s. Now everyone had a job. All worked to support the war effort. Radio factories made radar equipment. Motor works made tanks and aircraft. Woollen mills made uniforms. Many factories worked seven days a week.

In 1941 the managers of one coal-mine announced that every miner would be expected to work on Sunday morning and through the week. This was 'to help in the NATIONAL EMERGENCY. Every man is expected to pull his weight.' A serious shortage of coal later forced the government to recruit some young men into the coal-mines instead of into the armed forces.

As in the First World War, women did many of the jobs that had previously been done by men. One woman said she worked from seven in the morning till seven at night and the men 'thought it was strange to have a woman driving a crane because it was so big'.

Workers in the big cities had to learn to live with air raids every

With so many men away fighting, volunteers were required to help farmers around the country bring in their harvests.

Women drivers became a familiar sight during the Second World War.

night. This was especially hard on people who worked as air raid wardens at night and at a factory or office during the day. They often had to walk to work along roads riddled with craters from the bombs which had been dropped the night before. Many of the men joined the Home Guard and trained as volunteer soldiers after work.

Farmers grew as much food as possible from their land. They were helped by 100,000 Land Army girls who had volunteered to work on the land. The work was hard. Many city girls found it odd to live and work a long way away from the towns. Many were horrified by the primitive living conditions. They often had to do without electricity, flush toilets and hot tap water.

When the War ended in 1945, people looked forward to a new Britain. They wanted a fresh start with equality for all and an end to the poverty and

Nita Marcus, a 27-year-old ambulance driver in London during the Second World War, described how dangerous this job could be:
'One of our ambulances . . . went down to Surrey Docks, through flames meeting from each side of the road (where our next ambulance two minutes later could not get through) and picked up five casualties, including one woman who had just had a baby. Sparks and fragments kept falling on them – they beat them off their trousers . . . and came back another way past a wall that collapsed just behind them.'

Blazing fires kept volunteer firefighters busy when British cities were bombed during the Second World War.

unemployment of the 1930s. New laws gave them greater security in their jobs and the right to unemployment benefit. Better working conditions were also introduced. People worked shorter hours, enjoyed longer holidays and earned higher pay. By the 1970s, most people worked a forty-hour, five-day week.

The coming of the Welfare State also meant a big increase in the number of jobs in government and council offices. More and

> *'When I returned to England after the war I didn't know what I wanted to do. I was taken on by a large firm in the Midlands, at a wage of £5 a week. At that time, manufacturing firms were returning to the production of pre-war goods, after years of producing munitions and other goods for the war.'*
>
> Bill, a RAF officer, returning from the War in 1946.

This typist is working from a Dictaphone: she listens to a tape of dictation and types what she hears.

more people did office work instead of toiling in a factory. Wages rose because there was a shortage of labour.

After the Second World War many people moved to Britain from Commonwealth countries such as Jamaica or India. They saw Britain as a country that was wealthier than their own, with more jobs available. When they arrived many British employers gave them work that other people would not do because it was too low-paid. But immigrants would often be earning more than they were used to, even though their jobs tended to be uninteresting, such as cleaning or working in hospitals or in public transport.

In 1957 the Conservative prime minister, Harold Macmillan, made a very famous speech at Bedford. *'Most of our people have never had it so good. Go around the country . . . and you will see a state of prosperity such as we have never had in my lifetime – nor indeed ever in the history of the country.'*

There were big improvements in factory working conditions. In 1947 most coal-mines were still without pithead baths. Much of the coal was still cut by hand. But in the next fifteen years the National Coal Board spent millions of pounds on new equipment. Mines became safer and pleasanter places in which to work and the accident rate fell by two-thirds.

Thousands of Commonwealth immigrants found work in Britain in the 1950s.

6 IN RECENT YEARS

In recent years governments have passed many laws to help people at work. These include laws to control health and safety and to protect workers against unfair dismissal. The Equal Pay Act of 1970 gave women the right to equal pay for equal work. The widespread employment of women in many different types of jobs has probably been the most striking change at work in the last thirty years. It was unusual in 1960 to see women doctors, dentists, lawyers, engineers and bus drivers.

There have been other major changes as well. Fewer coal-miners are needed nowadays because coal can be taken from the ground using machinery. Energy can also be supplied from gas, oil and nuclear power, so less coal is used.

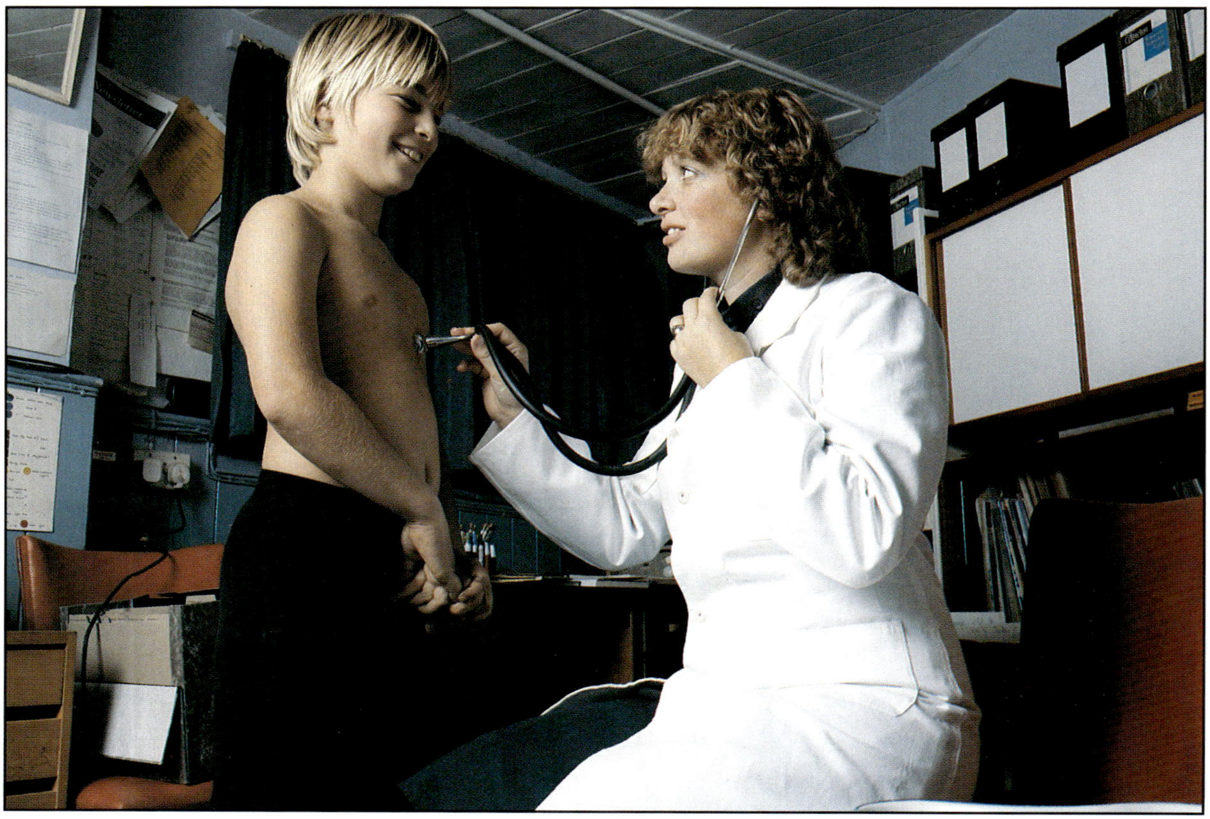

Women now have the chance to work in professions that used to employ only men.

Machines like the combine harvester reduce the need for farm labourers.

Railway workers have lost their jobs because fewer people travel by rail nowadays. Also, because of automation, not so many people are needed to operate the railways.

Fewer farm workers are employed because farmers have bought tractors and other labour-saving machines instead. The factories which made these products and machines did well in the 1960s. New jobs have been created in the gas, oil and electricity industries as well

> *'I mean you go into a field today and you stand at one side and you plough until you get to the other side. There's no skill attached to it now. I mean, the youngsters they really don't know what ploughing is, not in comparison with the old days.'*
>
> Len Sharman, Suffolk farm worker, on the BBC Television programme *All Our Working Lives: Farming*, 1984

This production line uses no human workers – only robots.

as in factories making cars and tractors.

The decline of the coal-mining, steel, textile and shipbuilding industries brought fresh unemployment to the North in the 1970s and 1980s. It was even more worrying when workers began to lose their jobs in the newer industries as well. Some of

> Will Paynter summed up the changes on the BBC Television programme *All Our Working Lives: Coal* in 1984.
> *'Coal-mining today is vastly different to what it was when I started in the pits back in 1917. Today men are working under a steel canopy with the kind of roof supports that are now in existence. The picks and hatchets are gone. It's the machines that cut and load the coal on the conveyors that convey to the pit. And on the surface you've got the same kind of development. It is an entirely different industry. It is more like a factory.'*

the factories making cars and television sets had to close down because they could not compete with factories making the same goods in other parts of the world.

Another reason for the rise in unemployment has been the use of automation at work. Robots have taken the place of many skilled workers. As a result, older workers no longer have the chance to use the skills they learned when they first went out to work.

Workers in other industries have also learned to use computers as part of their work. Many have jobs in service industries, such as banking and the leisure and tourist trades. Growing numbers of people do much of their work at home. They use computers, fax machines and the telephone to keep in touch with their employers. In the future, perhaps, most people's homes will be their places of work. Conditions at work will then depend on employees and not on employers.

Office workers, nowadays, have the use of telephones, calculators, fax machines and computers.

GLOSSARY

Automation Machinery which works on its own without needing the constant attention of a worker.

Compensation Money paid to someone to make up for loss or injury.

Depression When farms and factories find it hard to sell goods, and prices fall, causing firms to go out of business with the loss of many jobs.

Dole (or Unemployment Benefit) Money paid by the government to people out of work.

Equal pay When men and women are paid the same for doing the same work.

Exploit To take advantage of someone or something.

Farthing An old British coin worth less than ¼p.

Fax machine A machine that can send printed messages along telephone lines.

Ganger A child farm worker in a 'gang' which was hired out to farmers to do jobs, such as sowing and hoeing.

Hiring fair A special market where employers could go to choose workers who were offering their services as employees.

Manual workers People who work mainly with their hands.

Noisome Unpleasant and often harmful.

Protective clothing Special clothes, such as hard hats, goggles and heavy boots, worn by workers to protect themselves from injury.

Radar A method used to locate distant objects, such as ships or aircraft.

Sovereign A gold coin worth £1.

Sweatshop A small, back street factory or workroom where workers, very often women and children, were employed at the beginning of this century, to make goods for very low rates of pay.

Toil Hard or exhausting work.

Welfare State When the government takes responsibility for the well-being and welfare of the people.

IMPORTANT DATES

1901 Factory and Workshop Act made twelve years the minimum working age for children in factories
1909 First Labour Exchanges helped people get jobs
1911 National Insurance scheme helped workers in some industries to get unemployment benefit when they lost their jobs.
Half day closing for shopworkers introduced.
1926 General Strike
1929 Wall Street Crash in USA started a world-wide depression in industry and agriculture
1938 Holidays with Pay Act
1939 Women's Land Army formed at the start of the Second World War
1946 National Insurance Act made unemployment benefit available for all workers
1970 Equal Pay Act passed, to guarantee women equal pay for equal work (came into effect in 1975)

BOOKS TO READ

Behind the Main Street by Kenneth Hudson (The Bodley Head, 1982)
Finding Out About Edwardian Britain by Michael Rawcliffe (Batsford, 1989)
How We Used To Live, 1902–1926 by Freda Kelsall (A & C Black, 1985)
How We Used To Live, 1954–1970 by Freda Kelsall (A & C Black, 1987)
Spotlight on the Interwar Years by Michael Gibson (Wayland, 1986)
Timeline: Nursing by Erica Holley (Dryad Press, 1987)
Working Lives: Shops by Cherry Gilchrist (Batsford, 1987)
Working Lives: The Coal Mines by Nathaniel Harris (Batsford, 1987)
Working Lives: The Railway Industry by Betty Williams (Batsford, 1987)
Working Lives: The Textile Industry by Judy Slinn (Batsford, 1987)

PICTURE ACKNOWLEDGEMENTS

The publishers would like to thank the following for supplying the photographs in this book: Cadbury's 5 (bottom); E T Archives cover, 4, 10, 21, 22; Mary Evans Picture Library 6, 9, 11, 16 (bottom); Hulton Picture Library 12, 17 (both), 18, 19 (bottom), 24; Imperial War Museum 14, 15, 23; Billie Love 13, 16 (top), 20 (top); The Mansell Collection 7, 20 (bottom); Topham 5 (bottom), 8, 25, 29; Wayland 5 (top), 19 (top), 26, 27, 28.

INDEX

ACKNOWLEDGEMENTS

The publishers would like to thank William Heinemann Ltd for granting permission to quote from *English Journey* by J B Priestley.